OHIO *Simply Beautiful*

Photography by RANDALL LEE SCHIEBER

FARCOUNTRY
PRESS

RIGHT: Sylvan Pond in Cuyahoga
Valley National Park.

FRONT COVER: Lanterman's Mill
at Mill Creek Metro Park,
Mahoning County.

BACK COVER: Brandywine Falls
in Summit County.

TITLE PAGE: Hocking Hills State Park.

ISBN 1-56037-239-7
Photographs © Randall Lee Schieber
© 2003 Farcountry Press

For more information on our books write:
Farcountry Press, P.O. Box 5630, Helena,
MT 59604 or call: (800) 654-1105 or visit
www.montanamagazine.com

Created, produced, and designed in the
United States.
Printed in China

FOREWORD

Ohio is a state with much beauty, vitality and diversity. After all, this land has attracted residents since the prehistoric Adena people built their mysterious mounds, to the later white settlers who arrived in the 18th century and founded a state in 1803, forging the gateway that helped open up the West, and on to two more centuries of immigrants. Ohio is rich in its history, its cities, and its people (it's the birthplace of aviation, has contributed more presidents than any other state, and—yes—is even pretty hip, with its Rock and Roll Hall of Fame). It is rich in the diversity of its landscape, too. After twelve to fifteen years of hiking about and photographing it, I still am amazed to discover new and exciting places of interest. Whether it be the rivers and the lakes, or the hills and the valleys, little treasures keep turning up before me.

I have many favorite places that I like to explore. In the southeastern part of the state it is the Hocking Hills region, known for its rolling hills and valleys, and sandstone ledges and cliffs. In the northeast is the Cuyahoga Valley National Park, an amazingly scenic and well preserved valley that stretches between two of Ohio's largest metropolitan areas, Cleveland and Akron. In the north, it's Lake Erie, with its many picturesque lighthouses and islands. And to the south, it is the long and meandering Ohio river. In the Center of the state, in my hometown of Columbus, it is a unique little park, the Topiary Gardens (a "landscape of a painting of a landscape"), world renowned, and included in the Smithsonian's Archives of American Gardens.

In the springtime I love to go to the Hocking Hills, or the Wayne National Forest, when the trees regain their leaves and display them with such a passionate array of vibrant and iridescent greens. The buds on the trees begin to burst and bloom as if there were no tomorrow. When summer heat begins to build, I like to head to Lake Erie, and enjoy the scenic beauty from the land or the waves. In the fall I start to think of the leaves about to turn color, and make my way to the Cuyahoga Valley National Park to enjoy leaves in yellows and oranges, punctuated with sugar-maple reds so vibrant that the area rivals any New England landscape. In the winter, the Hocking Hills region often beckons me back, especially after a heavy snowfall. I'll find myself hoping for one more heavy snowfall before the arrival of spring, when several inches of snow and ice cover the sandstone formations, and weigh heavy on branches of hemlock and pine. I feel privileged to bear witness to such scenes of awesome and stunning beauty.

I've been truly fortunate to be able to take my passion, photography, and turn it into my profession. It has brought me into contact with so many interesting people, and given me the opportunity to visit and explore so many wonderful places. I hope that, with this book of photographs, both visitors and residents will discover and rediscover the wonder that is Ohio.

—Randall Lee Schieber

ABOVE: Pelts from beavers like this creature once had the French and the British fighting over Ohio.
JIM ROETZEL

FACING PAGE: A pleasant trail today, long ago a towpath for the Ohio & Erie Canal.

LEFT: Day begins at Hudson's Hudson Springs Park.

BELOW: The Circleville Pumpkin Show, first among its peers.

LEFT: Seat of an empire: Bob Evans Farm at Rio Grande.

BELOW: Cottontail rabbits delight in forests and lawns throughout the state.
JIM ROETZEL

FOLLOWING PAGE: Business and government mix downtown in Columbus, the state capital straddling the Scioto River.

LEFT: Barn red amidst early-autumn color near Fredericktown.

BELOW: Below that mist, Tinkers Creek Gorge offers serious paddling for experienced canoeists.

ABOVE: Re-enactors at Put-in-Bay on South Bass Island honor Admiral Oliver Hazard Perry's September 1813 victory over the British, in the War of 1812's Battle of Lake Erie.

RIGHT: The *W.P. Snyder, Jr.,* launched in 1918 and the nation's only surviving coal-fired, steam-powered sternwheel towboat, is part of the Ohio River Museum at Marietta.

ABOVE: A familiar silhouette in Buck Creek State Park.

LEFT: Cincinnati's Union Terminal began serving train passengers seven decades ago; today the Art Deco treasure is home to Cincinnati History Museum, Cincinnati Historical Society, the Museum of Natural History & Science, and Robert D. Lindner Family OMNIMAX Theater.

RIGHT: Clifton Gorge on the Little Miami State Scenic River.

BELOW: In downtown Columbus's Old Deaf School Park, The Topiary Garden portrays George Seurat's painting *A Sunday Afternoon on the Island of La Grande Jatte* in shaped and trimmed yew trees.

FACING PAGE: The wheat is in on a Wayne County Amish farm.

LEFT: Wood ducks, the most abundant duck in the eastern United States.
JIM ROETZEL

BELOW: At Schoenbrunn State Memorial near New Philadelphia, reconstructed log buildings and exhibits tell of the Moravian church mission among the Delaware Indians that began in 1772.

RIGHT: Flemish-style Mac-O-Chee Castle near West Liberty dates from 1879, and today exhibits European and American tapestries, furniture, and works of art.

BELOW: Artist Malcolm Cochran's "Field of Corn" at Dublin honors the city's founding as a farming community.

ABOVE: Perhaps this photographer has a little treat to offer?

LEFT: Creek Road Bridge is one of Ashtabula County's sixteen covered bridges.

FOLLOWING PAGE: Holmes County has one of the nation's larger concentrations of Amish farms.

LEFT: Franklin Park Conservatory Botanical Garden in Columbus presents natural habitats from around the world.

BELOW: Extravagant turkey-tail mushrooms grow among ragworts.

ABOVE: Sunrise near Hoover Dam at Westerville.

RIGHT: Just paddlin' along at Buck Creek State Park.

Dawes Arboretum, near Newark, was founded in 1929, and today covers nearly 1200 acres of plantings and natural areas.

LEFT: Mansfield's Kingwood Center, once a private estate, delights garden- and flower-lovers from around the world.

RIGHT: Fruit of the vine near Vermilion.

BELOW: This Amish lad's shirt is in a traditional color.

FACING PAGE: The Paulding County Courthouse, at Paulding.

BELOW: Hale Farm & Village at Bath, situated in imaginary but fact-based Wheatfield Township, takes visitors back to life in the Western Reserve of 1848.

ABOVE: Pickaway County sunflowers—a cash crop that creates cheerful fields.

LEFT: Official symbols of the Buckeye State's first two hundred years decorate at least one barn in each of Ohio's eighty-eight counties.

RIGHT: Jack Frost has left his signature on Clark County.

BELOW: Frosted-leaf mosaic.

ABOVE: This young Cooper's hawk does most of its hunting hidden in the forest. JIM ROETZEL

LEFT: Spring green at The Topiary Garden, Columbus.

43

RIGHT: From its opening 1866 until 1984, this Ohio River bridge was simply called the Cincinnati and Covington Bridge; then it was renamed John A. Roebling Suspension Bridge to honor its designer.

BELOW: Grand Lake at St. Mary State Park is a grand place to be an angler's helper.

ABOVE: Dedicated in 1871 to honor early Cincinnati businessman Tyler Davidson, this city landmark gave the name to Fountain Square.

LEFT: Painted turtles, alert to the possibility of a tasty airborne snack. JIM ROETZEL

FAR LEFT: Distinctive and appropriate design at Canton's Pro Football Hall of Fame.

RIGHT: Jefferson County's Honeycake Winery.

BELOW: Cleveland Botanical Garden close up.

ABOVE: Gallipolis was founded in 1790 by French immigrants still supporting their king after the French Revolution.

LEFT: The Ohio Central Railroad puffs its way through Sugar Creek.

RIGHT: Tidy, busy Amish farms.

BELOW: Canada geese pause in central Ohio wetlands during their southerly migration.

ABOVE: The Rock and Roll Hall of Fame and Museum, in Cleveland, sports architecture as exuberant as its collections.

LEFT: At The Great Lakes Historical Society's Inland Seas Maritime Museum, Vermilion, stands this 1991 replica of the local lighthouse that served Lake Erie shipping beginning in 1877, and was razed in 1929.

FACING PAGE: Hocking Hills State Park offers cool respite on even the muggiest summer afternoons.

RIGHT: A West Virginia white butterfly's camouflage at work while it perches on a trillium blossom. JIM ROETZEL

BELOW: Great heron in Crane Creek State Park, Ottawa County.

ABOVE: Raccoons are everywhere—happily adaptable to living among humans and those useful garbage cans. JIM ROETZEL

LEFT: Sundown over Lake Erie, seen from Headlands Beach State Park in Lake County.

ABOVE: Leatherlips, a Ralph Helmick sculpture at Dublin, recalls the Delaware Indian chief who was killed by his tribe when he refused to fight white settlers.

RIGHT: Cleveland's Harbor Fest.

LEFT: Go, Bucks! at Ohio State University on an autumn afternoon.

BELOW: Azaleas afire in Toledo Botanical Gardens.

Alum Creek State Park,
Delaware County.

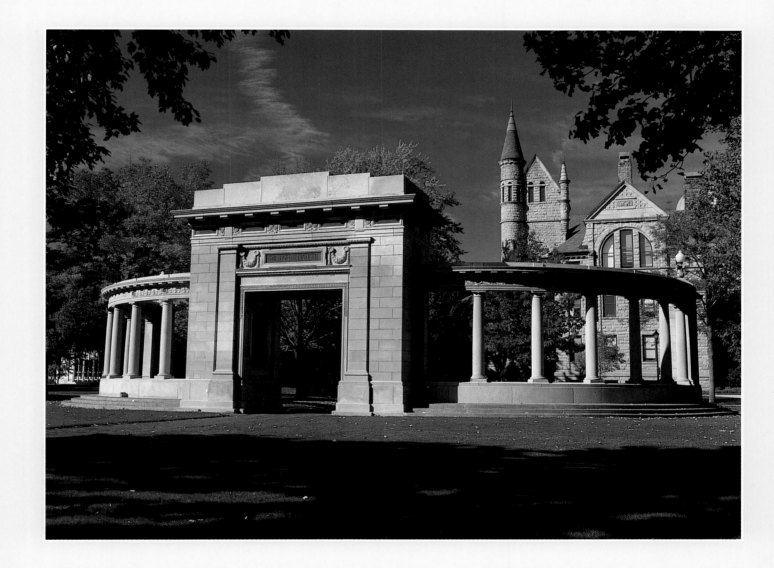

ABOVE: Oberlin, and Oberlin College (seen above), were both founded in 1833.

LEFT: Gallipolis and the Ohio River.

ABOVE: Nelson-Kennedy Ledges State Park, Portage County.

RIGHT: Reflections of Gahanna Woods State Nature Preserve.

ABOVE: Looking for The Longaberger Company headquarters in Dresden? —here's home for the nation's premier handcrafted-basket company.

RIGHT: This view, looking over the Ohio State Fair to the Columbus skyline, requires specially allowed access to the roof of Ohio Historical Society.

RIGHT: Tulip time for Schiller Park in the German Village section of Columbus.

BELOW: East Liverpool's 126' Alumni Clock Tower marks the former site of Central School.

LEFT: On Catawba Island, Lake Erie.

BELOW: Eastern coyotes live in open forest lands. JIM ROETZEL

RIGHT: Wind-power for Bob Evans' farm, Rio Grande.

BELOW: The state capitol's rotunda following renovation.

The stout-hearted Fairport
Harbor Lighthouse in
Lake County.

ABOVE: A stormy sunset for Catawba Island and Ohio's Great Lake.

LEFT: The Flats area of Cleveland hosts festivals and special events year-around.

RIGHT: Troy's Miami County Courthouse, built in 1888, sports a cast iron dome modeled on that of the U.S. Capitol.

BELOW: Cedar Falls is one of Hocking Hills State Park's many beauties.

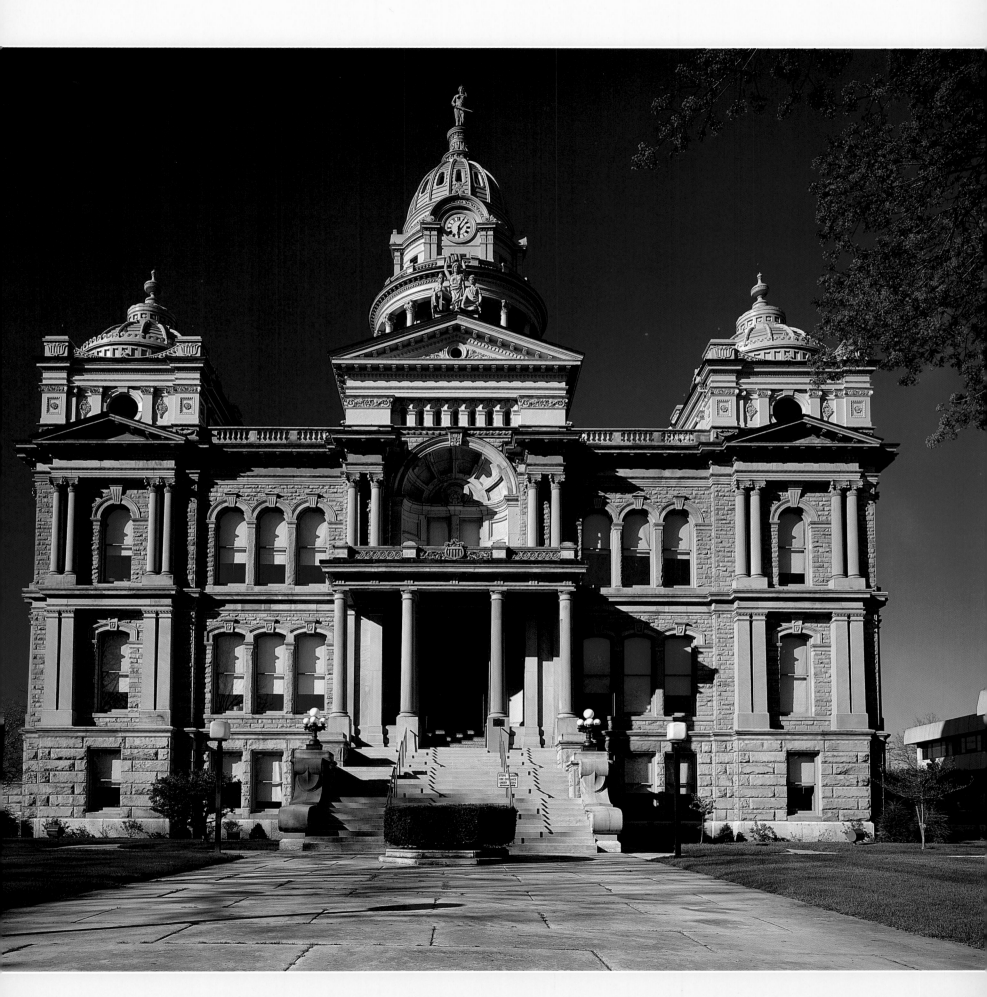

LEFT: Lake Hope, Vinton County, adorned with water lilies.

BELOW: Whimsy abounded during Cincinnati's Big Pig Gig.

RIGHT: A Dayton celebration lights up the Great Miami River.

BELOW: Ohio's many species of hardwoods make autumn a carnival of brilliant color.

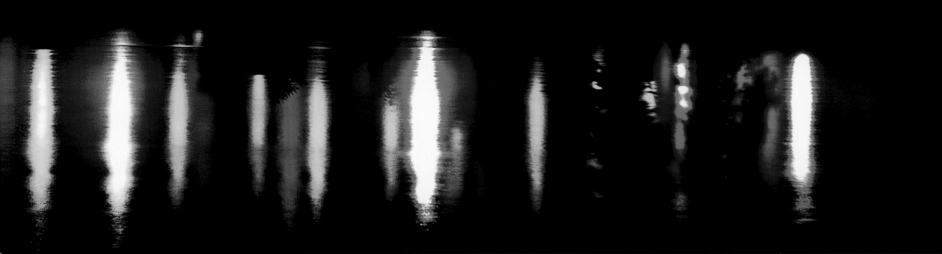

LEFT: Brandywine Falls rushes through autumn woods.

BELOW: Northern orioles, nicknamed "Baltimore," build their distinctive nests in Ohio shade trees.
JIM ROETZEL

RIGHT: What summer-only visitors to southern Ohio's Old Man's Cave area miss enjoying.

BELOW: Ohio's state bird, the northern cardinal, raises its loud, clear song year-around.
JIM ROETZEL

LEFT: A fox squirrel cruises for its winter treat. JIM ROETZEL

FAR LEFT: The sun seems to flatten as it drops into Lake Erie for the night.

BELOW: In Wapakoneta, hometown boy and first man to step onto the moon is honored at Neil Armstrong Air & Space Museum—along with other space pioneers including fellow Ohioan John Glenn.

RIGHT: The peaceful Inniswood Metro Gardens at Westerville.

BELOW: Dawes Arboretum.

ERECTED 1895

LEFT: The Trumbull County Courthouse has towered over Warren since 1895.

BELOW: A perfect way to enjoy Park of Roses in Columbus.

RIGHT: Author Louis Bromfield's beloved Malabar Farm near Mansfield was an early demonstrator of contour farming.

BELOW: King of the mountain in Muskingum County.

LEFT: Harvest-time sunset in Holmes County.

BELOW: Special day for a Holmes County lass.

RIGHT: Cincinnati skyline.

BELOW: Great Serpent Mound in Adams County, effigy of a snake, stretches for 1,330 feet and rises three feet tall.

LEFT: The Muskingum River in the county that took its names.

BELOW: Bluebells in Scioto Trail State Park.

Fairport Harbor on Lake Erie.

BELOW: White-tailed deer have adapted too
well to living among human settlements.
JIM ROETZEL

LEFT: Twenty-five larger-than-life murals in downtown Steubenville tell the city's history.

BELOW: In Van Wert, the Peony Festival parade celebrates a cheery summer flower.

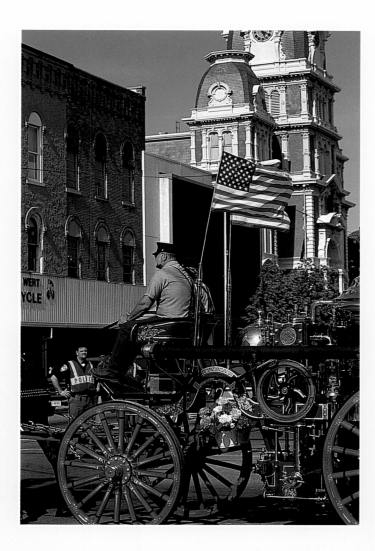

LEFT: "Powering up" at the Big Bear Balloon Festival, held in Grove City.

BELOW: Competition is fierce at Nelsonville's Paul Bunyan Show.

FACING PAGE: Outdoors amid the colors, Cleveland Botanical Garden.

BELOW: Classic farm equipment like these, and pioneer farm homes and equipment, are on exhibit at AuGlaize Village near Defiance.

RIGHT: Wind, water, and winter have sculpted the exposed sandstone cliffs of Nelson-Kennedy Ledges State Park near Newbury.

BELOW: A curious crowd in Licking County.

LEFT: Hune Covered Bridge in Wayne National Forest, Washington County.

BELOW: The Short North district in Columbus.

LEFT: This soybean field near Springfield contributes to Ohio's 180-million-bushel annual crop.

BELOW: Serious simian at the Columbus Zoo.

Riverboats gather at Ohio's first city, Marietta, for the Ohio River Sternwheel Festival.